DICTIONARY

OF THE

AFRICAN METHODIST EPISCOPAL CHURCH

Volume 1

Since 1787

Dr. Eric L. Brown

"I would have fainted unless, I had believed to see the goodness of the Lord in the land of the living.
Wait, on the Lord, be of good courage, And he will strengthen thy heart, Wait, I say on the Lord!"

Psalm 27:13-14 NKJV

ENDORSEMENTS

"I am most pleased to endorse" A Dictionary of the African Methodist Episcopal Church, Volume 1 **authored by The Reverend Dr. Eric L. Brown. Dr. Brown has served as a thoughtful and caring Shepherd of "God's people" who now serves most ably as a Presiding Elder, Supervising Pastors and Ministers.**

Dr. Brown's education, experience and leadership equip him uniquely for this work.

I commend and thank him for this outstanding contribution and recommend this text for Bishops, Presiding Elders, Pastors, Ministers and Candidates for Ministry, along with the Laity and our entire membership.

This is a treasure full of gold nuggets."

The Right Reverend McKinley Young,
Presiding Prelate, Third Episcopal District African Methodist Episcopal Church.

"This AME lexicon from the experienced pen of Dr. Eric L. Brown will be a helpful companion to our volumes on liturgy, hymnody and discipline. It will aid both the clergy and the laity in the performance of important duties in worship, administration and the teaching of African Methodist Episcopal polity and doctrine. It is a timely and useful primer on who we are as AME's."

Dr. Dennis Clark Dickerson, *Retired Historiographer of the African Methodist Episcopal Church.*

"What a powerful and needed tool, which can be used for training or just greater knowledge. This is a must for clergy and lay alike. There is not one place where we can get information for any A.M.E. term or phrase. This document is an absolute must for anyone in the A.M.E. Church from the newest members to those who have been in the church for 60 or more years. Thank you for allowing God to use you to bless us."

Mrs. Cheryl Hammond Hopewell, *President of the Philadelphia Annual Conference Lay Organization, First Episcopal District African Methodist Episcopal Church.*

"I predict that Dr. Eric Brown's comprehensive A Dictionary of the African Methodist Episcopal Church, Volume 1, *will become the definitive dictionary that will enable more clarity and in-depth understanding of the knowledge contained in our* Doctrine and Discipline of the African Methodist Episcopal Church." *This volume presents a thorough listing and defining of organizational and worship terms used on all levels of African Methodism- local, presiding elder's district, annual conference, Episcopal District and Connectional. This Dictionary promotes and enhances an understanding of these terms. Furthermore, the style and format of this user-friendly text will be useful for the typical seminary student; studying African Methodist Episcopal Church History and Polity. I look forward to using this* Dictionary of the African Methodist Episcopal Church, Volume 1 *at Payne Theological Seminary and suggesting it to students."*

Reverend Betty Whitted Holley, *Ph.D., Professor of Environmental Ethics and African American Studies at Payne Theological Seminary and Presiding Elder of the Columbus & Springfield-Xenia Districts African Methodist Episcopal Church.*

"This is a timely literary work that will enhance the church of Richard and Sarah Allen for years to come. The challenge for us is to use it to enlighten the minds of our people."

Reverend Dr. Floyd W. Alexander, Sr., *Administrative Assistant to the Bishop of the Third Episcopal District of the African Methodist Episcopal Church.*

"Dr. Brown has compiled an exhaustive list of definitions that are germane to African Methodism. Many terms are commonly used but never fully understood. This work is a major enhancer to the new and seasoned members alike who seek to learn more about our great Zion and to speak the proper language of the church."

Dr. Eugene L. Schoolfield, II, *Pastor, St. James African Methodist Episcopal Church, Cleveland, Ohio*

A Dictionary of

The

African Methodist Episcopal Church

Copyright©2014

by Dr. Eric L. Brown

ISBN: 1494363704

ISBN: 13-9781494363703

Dr. Eric L. Brown

Post Office Box 17063

Pittsburgh, PA 15235

This book was printed in the United States of America.

To Order additional copies of this book contact:

www.amazon.com

TABLE OF CONTENTS

"So High a Calling, So Holy a Mission."

Daniel Alexander Payne

(1811-1893)

DEDICATION

To all those patriarchs and matriarchs of the faith who have made it possible for us to come to this very hour. They are looking down from the balcony of Heaven watching over me.

My grandmother, *Elsie Mae Brown*, who taught me how to love God and the African Methodist Episcopal Church. To my Godfather, **the *Reverend Simon Marsh*,** who was my mentor in ministry, he taught me the importance and joy of loving and serving God's people.

To *Bishop Richard Allen Hildebrand*, who saw something in me and sent me to Wilberforce University and paid my tuition.

Special Thanks to:

My wife, *Margo Allen Brown, who is my greatest fan and best critic* for her constant encouragement during this project.

Bishop McKinley Young, my Bishop and friend for his wisdom and guidance throughout this project.

My Administrative Aide, *Miss Shelly Brown*, for her many dedicated hours of typing this manuscript.

INTRODUCTION

There has long been a great need for a dictionary of organizational and worship terms that are widely used in the African Methodist Episcopal Church. As the oldest predominantly religious organism founded by persons of color as a result of the racial injustice that our fore-parents experienced at St. George's Methodist Church in November, 1787 in Philadelphia, Pennsylvania, we need and deserve our own dictionary.

The fact is that unique meanings and understandings have grown up over the years for many words and phrases that A.M.E.'s routinely use. Often it is preconceived within our fellowship that everyone at the local, Annual Conference and connectional levels of the denomination knows what the basic meaning of a commonly used term is or the specific connotation it holds for A.M.E.'s.

This dictionary has been compiled to facilitate communication among members by providing a succinct definition of the vocabulary we use in our life together as members of the African Methodist Episcopal Church.

If communication and understanding are improved, our worship and organizational experiences will have greater significance for all of us.

There are three presuppositions that undergird the plan of this book:

1. *Most of the organizational and worship terms used in the African Methodist Episcopal Church have meanings and nuances that are distinct to our denomination.*
2. *Many members of the African Methodist Episcopal Church have forgotten or were never informed about the distinctive character of our church and the way in which we talk about its customs and practices.*
3. *Many of today's members did not grow up within the African Methodist Episcopal Church.*

It is my prayer that this dictionary will commend itself to you. If it improves our shared understanding of the vocabulary of our denomination, it will have served its purpose. Through that enhanced understanding, it is hoped that the life and ministry in Christ we share together as members of the African Methodist Episcopal Church will be enriched.

A

Abandoned Property: The formal process of disposing the property and other assets of a local church when a congregation has disbanded and no longer continues to meet. As a result of all local church trustees hold all real and personal property in trust for the connection it must take the final action to dispose of the property.

Accessions: A new member added to the church.

Accountability: The quality or state of being accountable to a superior person or body.

Acolyte: One who assists the celebrant in the performing of liturgical rites. They usually lead the procession during worship and light the candles on the altar.

Acrostic: A literary device in which successive lines or verses begin with letters in the alphabetical order.

Active Membership: Those members of a local church who are in good and regular standing.

Administrative Assistant to the Bishop: An emissary selected by the presiding bishop of an episcopal district who is well versed in the administrative operations of the church. They are usually second in command of a district and serve as advisors to the bishop.

Admission to the Church: The act of one completing the new members training and being read into full membership into the African Methodist Episcopal Church.

Advent Wreath: A green wreath with two purple, one pink, and one blue candle, used during the celebration of advent in the church and in homes as we celebrate the birth of our Savior.

Advent: The name for the liturgical season that begins four Sundays/Weeks preceding Christmas Day.

Affiliate Member: A member of the African Methodist Episcopal Church who is temporarily residing in the vicinity of another church. They have all the rights and privileges of membership.

Agape: A Greek term for one of the four types of love in the Bible. It is often characterized as an in spite of love.

Alb: A vestment worn by clergy persons with a cincture around the waist.

Altar Cloth: A white cloth that covers the altar, which signifies the purity of Christ.

Altar Guild: A ministry of the local church with the responsibility of taking special care of the altar and all of its accessories.

Altar: The symbolic place of prayer where the sacraments are celebrated. African Methodist Episcopal Churches are distinguished by the presence of altars in our sanctuaries.

Allen, Flora: (1755-1801) The first wife of Richard Allen who preceded him in death.

Allen, Richard: The founder of the Free African Society (1787), also the founder and first elected and consecrated bishop of the African Methodist Episcopal Church (1816).

Allen, Sarah: The second wife of Richard Allen who aided him in the formation of the African Methodist Episcopal Church by organizing a group of women to mend the clothes and feed the itinerate preachers whom her husband sent out to extend the church.

Amen: Meaning it is so, or the end.

American Bible Society: An inter-confessional, non-denominational, non-profit group founded on May 11, 1816 in New York City, which publishes, distributes and translates the Bible and provides study aids to help people engage and study the Bible.

Annual Conference Delegate: An adult member of the local church who has been duly elected by secret ballot to represent the local congregation at a session of the annual conference.

Annual Conference Report: The statistical report of the labors of a pastor and congregation that is presented orally during the annual conference session.

Annual Conference Secretary: A member of the Annual Conference who has been elected to serve as the secretary. They are charged with the responsibility of acquiring and maintaining all of the records and documents relative to the annual conference.

Annual Conference: A geographical area of churches that meets at the call of the presiding bishop.

Annual Sermon: The Sermon that is preached by a seasoned itinerate elder at the opening of the annual conference.

Anthem: A specific form of Anglican Church music or more generally a song of celebration.

Anvil: The symbol of the African Methodist Episcopal Church, our founder Richard Allen preached his first sermon from behind an anvil in his blacksmith shop.

Apocrypha: Means hidden things in Greek. There are two categories of texts, which are included in some canonical versions of scripture, and texts that are not found in other biblical literature.

Apostle: One of a group made up especially of the twelve disciples chosen by Jesus to preach the gospel. They were sent out as missionaries by Jesus Christ to spread the word and extend the church.

Apostles' Creed/Affirmation of Faith: Developed between the second and ninth centuries as a baptismal creed for new Christians.

Apostolic Succession: The method whereby the ministry of the Christian Church is derived from the apostles by a continuous succession.

Appeal: A written charge against a pastor, bishop or leader in the African Methodist Episcopal Church who is believed to have violated the Doctrine and Discipline.

Appointment: A one-year assignment to serve as the pastor of a congregation .

Articles of Incorporation: A legal document that creates a corporation it is filed with the secretary of state by the founders of a corporation.

Articles of Religion: The official doctrinal statement of Methodism.

Asbury, Francis: (1745- 1816) Was one of the first two bishops of the Methodist Episcopal Church in the United States. He ordained Richard Allen as a bishop in 1816.

Ascension: Moving upwards, climbing and maneuvering.

Ash Wednesday: The first day of the liturgical season called Lent.

Assessment: The payments received from the local church to benefit the Annual Conference, Episcopal District and Connectional Church.

Assignment: Bishops of the African Methodist Episcopal Church do not receive appointments, they receive four-year assignments to Episcopal Districts by the Episcopal Committee and the said assignments are confirmed or ratified by the General Conference.

B

Bands: A meeting that precedes the Class meeting. They are comprised of all men or all women.

Baptism: Water baptism of new converts into the Christian Church. There are three modes: *sprinkling, pouring or immersion.*

Beatitudes: A set of teachings by Jesus that begin with blessed are and are found in Matthew 5.

Bench of Bishops: Often referred to as the Council of Bishops. It is comprised of all of the active and retired bishops of the church. The retired bishops are not permitted to vote on fiscal matters since they have no responsibility to report funds to the general church.

Benediction: The utterance of a blessing at the end of a worship celebration.

Benevolence: An act of extending charity to those in need.

Bible: A collection of sixty-six books, which we believe to be the divinely inspired word of God.

Biennial: Occurring or being done every two years. The word is used to describe the Connectional Meeting of the Lay Organization.

Bishop: Persons elected by the General Conference to exercise the Episcopacy. They must by the law of the church retire from active service at the General Conference nearest their 75th birthday.

Bishops, Female: The General Conference of 2000 met in Cincinnati, Ohio and elected the first female to the episcopacy, *Vashti Murphy McKenzie*. In 2004 the General Conference met in Indianapolis, Indiana and elected *Carolyn Tyler Guidry* and *Sarah Frances Taylor Davis*.

Blacksmith Shop: A place where horseshoes are made. This was also the first place of worship for Richard Allen and his followers in 1787. Richard Allen preached the first sermon using an anvil as a pulpit.

Blessing: The infusion of something with holiness, spirited, redemption and divine will.

Board of Examiners: A group of clergy persons whom all have earned at least the Master of Divinity degree from an Association of Theological Schools Accredited Institution who prepare candidates for ordination through providing instruction to them.

Book of Worship: A book containing various liturgies, prayers and consecration orders of services.

Book Steward: One who is responsible for the purchasing and selling of denominational literature within an episcopal district.

Boundaries: A specific area (i.e. *conference, episcopal district, presiding elder district).*

Bread: The symbol of the transubstantiated body of Christ that is shared by the believer during the sacrament of Holy Communion.

Brotherhood Movement: At the 1956 General Conference a group of single-minded clergypersons from across the length and breadth of the African Methodist Episcopal Church led the charge to reform the church for the better by instituting: The Episcopal District Budget and fiscal accountability.

Budget: An itemized summary of estimated or intended expenditures and a proposal for financing them.

C

Cabinet: A term referring the presiding elders council. They are the bishop's cabinet, as the local stewards are members of the pastor's cabinet.

Call to Preach: The acknowledgment of God's divine call to preach the Word and call sinners to repentance.

Call to Worship: A collection of scripture sentences that are used to call a congregation to worship.

Camp Baber: A campground in Cassopolis, Michigan named in honor of the 63rd Bishop of the church, Bishop George Wilburn Baber.

Candidate: A person who seeks membership, an office or an honor. In our church there are candidates for baptism, ordination and offices.

Canon: The books of the Bible recognized as having authority as Scripture and being accepted for use. The word canon comes from the Greek word meaning ruler or measuring rod.

Cassock: A long gown or vestment usually black in color, traditionally worn by Roman Catholic and Anglican clergy.

Cathedral of African Methodism: Metropolitan Church was founded in 1838 in Washington, D.C. It is known as the cathedral of African Methodism.

Catholic: The word means universal.

Celtic Cross: A symbol that combines a cross with a ring surrounding the intersection.

Chalice: A vessel that is used during communion containing the symbolic blood of our Lord and Savior Jesus Christ.

Chancel: The area in the sanctuary where the altar and communion table are located.

Chant: A method of singing parts of a worship service such as Psalms, canticles, litanies or other portions of the worship without the benefit of music.

Chapel: A small meditative room set aside for worship, other than the main sanctuary or worship center.

Chaplain: An ordained clergy person who ministers in a penal institution, a hospital, nursing home or the armed forces.

Charge, pastoral: The term given to a congregation when the Bishop assigns a clergy person to serve them for a one-year term.

Charges against a minister or lay member: The initial step in the process of beginning an investigation or trial of a lay member or minister. The AME Church has a detailed process for the investigations, trials and appeals of ordained ministers, local deacons and elders, licentiates and lay persons. *The Book of Discipline* lists those offenses for which charges can be made and the procedures for making them.

Charter: A legal document presented to a subordinate (*the local church*) group from the parent (*denomination*) body.

Chief Celebrant: The senior most person in rank present during the celebration of a sacrament is the chief celebrant.

Choir: An organized musical ministry in the church that provides music during worship celebrations.

Choral Selection: A musical selection presented by a group during a worship experience.

Christ Candle: The large white candle used on Christmas Eve or on Christmas Day or both. The Christ candle is often the candle located in the center of the Advent wreath.

Christian Education: A ministry of the church that seeks to empower members with skills and tools to help them live fruitful Christian lives to the glory of God.

Christian Recorder: The official news organ of the African Methodist Episcopal Church. It was founded in 1889. It has had 21 editors in its history.

Christian Social Action: The Act of the being involved in socio-political issues that impact the people that we serve.

Christian: A person who believes in Jesus Christ; a person who exemplifies in their life, the teachings of Christ; believers were first called Christians at Antioch. (Acts 11:26)

Christmas Conference: The name given to the conference at which the Methodist Episcopal Church in America was formally organized. The conference began on December 24, 1784 and lasted until January 2nd or 3rd, 1785 at the Lovely Lane Chapel in Baltimore, Maryland.

Church Conference: The convening of a meeting of all of the members in a specific congregation to transact the temporal business of the church. The pastor serves as the presiding officer and is the only person duly qualified to call a church conference.

Church Membership: When one desires to flee the wrath of the world and comes forward during an invitation to discipleship, expressing their desire to become a member of the body of Christ through the local church.

Church School Convention: A gathering of all the churches on a presiding elder's district for the purpose of enhancing the church schools throughout the district.

Church School: A ministry of Bible teaching and learning that is the foundation of the educational ministry of the church.

Cincture: A rope or band placed around the waist of a cassock or alb. Generally, it is the same color as the garment over which it is worn, but it may be the liturgical color of the season.

Circuit Rider: A term used to describe pioneers of our denomination who rode on horseback to serve several congregations.

Circuit: Two or more local churches joined together for pastoral supervision.

Class Dues: The amount of money collected by a class leader for the support of the pastor and the spreading of the gospel of Jesus Christ.

Class Leader: A person who is selected by the pastor to serve as a lay sub pastor in a local congregation.

Class: The membership in a local congregation divided into small groups.

Cluster: A group of churches that meet together at the call of the presiding elder for the purpose of holding a joint quarterly conference.

Coker, Daniel: The first elected Bishop of the African Methodist Episcopal Church, who resigned to make way for Richard Allen to be the first elected and consecrated Bishop to serve.

Collect: A short prayer with a very precise form. It contains an address to God referring to some attribute of God, a petition relation to that attribute, a reference to the desired result of the petition, and closing words stating that the prayer is through Jesus Christ.

Colleges: The African Methodist Episcopal Church owns and operates the following colleges: *Wilberforce University (1856), Allen University (1880), Edward Waters College (1881), Paul Quinn College (1881), Morris Brown College (1885), Shorter College (1886), Wilberforce Community College (1908), Monrovia College, A.M.E. University (1994).*

Colors, Liturgical: The colors symbolizing the days and seasons of the Christian Year, used for stoles and other vestments, altar cloths and other paraments and church decorations. The liturgical colors are as follows: *Advent, Purple; Christmas, White; Season After Epiphany, White; Lent, Purple; Easter, White; Pentecost, Red, Ordinary Time, Green.*

Communion: A term used to describe the Holy Eucharist or the Lord's Supper. It also refers to a denomination within the body of Christ. The African Methodist Episcopal Church is a communion. The National Council of Churches of Christ is often referred to as an organization of Christian communions.

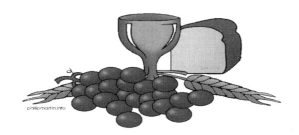

Conferences: The African Methodist Episcopal Church has five conferences: *General, Annual, District, Quarterly and Church.*

Conference Membership: The historic number of members that churches once had that is used to establish the boundaries of an annual conference.

Confession of Faith: According to Romans 10:9,10 if you confess with your mouth the Lord Jesus and believe in your heart that God raised Jesus from the dead, you shall be saved.

Confirm: To authenticate or empower a person to discharge a duty.

Confirmation of Stewards: After the pastor nominates the stewards they cannot or should not officially function as stewards until they are confirmed by a vote of the quarterly conference.

Connection: The term frequently used to refer to the entire organization of the African Methodist Episcopal Church.

Connectional Council: A group of clergy persons who work to ensure that the church has the proper leadership. The presidency of the council alternates between Northern and Southern Episcopal Districts.

Consecration: The act of laying hands on a deaconess or a bishop setting them aside for a Holy Office and work in the church.

Consubstantiation: A doctrine of the Eucharist affirming that Christ's body and blood substantially coexist with the consecration of the bread and wine.

Conversion: The act of being born spiritually into the Kingdom of God. A change in behavior from secular to spiritual.

Council of Bishops: The executive branch consisting of all the bishops and familiarly called the Bishops Council of the African Methodist Episcopal Church.

Course of Study: A prescribed curriculum for ministry candidates that is taught by the members of the Board of Examiners.

Covenant: An agreement or vow made between church members to defend and support the faith and doctrines of the church.

Crèche: A nativity scene representing the stable in Bethlehem with the Christ child, Mary and Joseph. Many crèches also have figures of the shepherds, the wise men and various animals.

Credentials: An official document certifying the right of an individual to act as a member, or delegate of this official body.

Creed: A brief, authoritative statement of religious belief. For example: The Apostle's Creed and the Nicene Creed.

Cremation: The burning of the body of a deceased person. It is not commonly viewed as a Christian burial.

Love the Lord with all your heart, amen.

D

Deacon: The first of two ministerial orders/ordination of the AME Church. There are itinerate *(travelling)* and local *(stationary)* deacons.

Deaconess: A woman selected by the pastor and Official board and consecrated by the Bishop. Her duties are to cheer the fallen, minister to the hungry, homeless, imprisoned and institutionalized.

Dean: The term given to the person who is in charge of the developing and administering the course of study to potential candidates for ordination.

Decalogue: The Ten Commandments. A part of the liturgy of the AME Church derived from Exodus 20:1-17.

Deed: A legal document that describes the dimensions of a parcel of land and lists the legal owner.

Delegate: A person who has been duly elected by a body to represent them at a conference: *General Conference, Annual Conference, District Conference, Lay Biennial, WMS Quadrennial, etc.*

Denomination: The body of persons or the organization formed around a particular set of religious beliefs or structure or type of government.

Director of Lay Activities (DOLA): A person who serves at the local, episcopal district or connectional level as the resource development persons for the lay organization.

Disciple: A follower of Jesus. During the biblical days Jesus chose a group of twelve.

Discipleship: The active living of the individual Christian in accordance with the teachings of Jesus Christ, that is, being as effective a disciple of Christ as possible.

Disciplinary Questions: The questions asked at the closing business session of the annual conference by the presiding bishop and answered by the conference secretary. This term also refers to the questions that the presiding elder asks at a quarterly conference.

Discipline: A term with three distinct meanings: Early Methodists acquired a reputation for having strict patterns and rules for regulating their daily spiritual lives. This "discipline" became characteristic of the movement in its early years in England and the United States:

Second, the word related to constancy of practice and organizational form that has been maintained throughout the years.

Third, The Discipline is the shortened, commonly used name for the book containing the law, doctrine, the administrative and organizational guidelines for the denomination.

District Conference: The meeting held to conduct necessary work of the district. It meets at the call of the presiding elder and examines candidates for ministry and affirms or rejects them for further service.

District Coordinator/Consultant: The title given to the Presiding Elder's spouse, who assists the elder in the discharge of their respective duties.

District, Episcopal: A geographical portion of the global church presided over by a Bishop who is nominated to serve by the Episcopal Committee and ratified by the delegates of the General Conference.

District, Presiding Elder: A geographical portion of the annual conference presided over by the presiding elder, who is appointed annually by the presiding bishop.

Doctrine: A Latin word *doctrina* a codification of beliefs or a body of teachings or instructions.

Dogma: A principle or set of principles laid down by an authority as incontrovertibly true.

Dollar Money: The method of denominational financing that the general budget replaced

Dossal: A drapery hanging behind and above the Lord's table (*communion table*).

Doxology: A short statement of praise, glory and thanksgiving to God. It is often a short hymn designed to be sung by the worshiping congregation. The doxology most familiar to AME's is the hymn *"Old 100th "* with the opening line, *"Praise God from who all blessings flow."*

E

Easter Season: The season fifty days from Easter to Pentecost Day.

Easter Vigil: A service beginning on Saturday night and lasting until early Easter morning. The service may be held before dawn on Easter Sunday morning. The principal portions of the Easter Vigil are:

1. *The Service of Light*
2. *The Service of the Bread and Cup*
3. *The Service of the Water*
4. *The Service of the Word*

Easter: The day in the Christian calendar that celebrates the resurrection of Jesus Christ. Easter is the most important day in the calendar. It is celebrated on the first Sunday after the full moon or after March 21; therefore the date varies from March 22 to April 25.

Ecumenical: From the Greek word meaning the whole inhabited earth. It involves dialogue and joint action among various sectors of the Christian community.

Education Night: During the Annual Conferences of the Education Supporting District: 1-13, they receive special offerings for the benefit of our educational institutions.

Eight Year Law: The General Conference mandated that no active Bishop shall serve in any episcopal district more than eight years.

Elder: The name given to the highest order in ordained ministry in the African Methodist Episcopal Church. Elders are clergy persons who have completed their formal preparation for ministry, either through the board of examiners training or theological seminary.

Elected and Consecrated: A term that is ascribed to all of the bishops of the African Methodist Episcopal Church since 1816.

Elements: The term used to refer to the bread and wine used in the Sacrament of the Lord's Supper.

Epiphany: January 6, which marks the end of the Christmas Season. In the Western Church, Epiphany Day is marked with the observance of the arrival of the wise men. The liturgical color for Epiphany is *White*.

Episcopacy: Refers to the office of Bishop. It also refers to the system of church government in which bishops serve as general superintendents.

Episcopal Address: A religious, socio-political statement written by several contributing authors that is presented at the General Conference every four years by one of the bishops of the church. It can be characterized as the state of the church and country report for the connection.

Episcopal District: A geographical area over-which an active bishop presides.

Episcopal District Administration: The funds received from the local church that assist in the operation of the Episcopal District obligations, such as office, support staff, housing for the Episcopal family. The Doctrine and Discipline is clear that it should not exceed 35% of the General Budget unless the District has an Educational Institution or a special project approved by the General Conference.

Episcopal Fund: The general fund that provides for the salaries and expenses of the bishops of the church.

Episcopal Headquarters: The official office of the presiding bishop within their respective episcopal district.

Episcopal Lay President: The person who is elected by the laity of an episcopal district to give leadership to the endeavors of the laity.

Episcopal Residence: The residence is provided for each active bishop within the confines of their Episcopal District to which they are assigned. The members of the respective episcopal district maintain it.

Episcopal Supervisor: The term referring to the spouse of the presiding bishop who typically oversees the work of the Women's Missionary Society within a respective episcopal district.

Episcopal W.M.S. President: The person who is appointed by the bishop and episcopal supervisor to give leadership to the district mission efforts.

Epistle: A letter, especially a formal one. One of the apostolic letters in the New Testament.

Epworth: A small town in northeast Lincolnshire, England, that was the birthplace of John and Charles Wesley. Their father, Samuel Wesley was the Church of England rector of the Epworth parish. The Wesley home, the Epworth rectory still stands and is a focal point for Methodists when visiting there.

Eschatology: The study of last or final things, as death, the end of the age.

Eulogist: The clergyperson who delivers a primary message during a funeral.

Evangelism: The action of spreading the gospel in new and creative ways.

Evangelist: An individual who actively seeks to bring others into a vital relationship with Jesus Christ. They are licensed preachers and receive their evangelist certificate annually from the hand of the presiding bishop at the bishops discretion.

Exhorter: A person who has been examined by the quarterly conference who employs their gifts and talents as a teacher, leading study groups and conducting prayer services.

F

Faith: According to Hebrews 11, it is the substance of things hoped for and the evidence of things not seen.

Fiscal Year: Determined by the General Conference June 1 through May 31.

Font, baptismal: A special container used to hold the water for the Sacrament of Baptism. It is usually inside the chancel railing.

Founding Date of the Denomination: The date of the organization of the first denomination founded by blacks for blacks is 1816. Prior to that there were several congregations with a loose affiliation. Although we celebrate the 1787 walk out of St. Georges'.

Free African Society: In November, 1787 when Richard Allen, Absalom Jones and their cohorts were pulled from their knees by the ushers at St. Georges' Church in Philadelphia, they walked out and started the FAS, which served as a mutual aide society to assist members in times of sickness and to care for widows and orphans.

Full Connection, Minister In: A historic phrase within the African Methodist Episcopal Church denoting a person who is an ordained itinerate elder and a member of an Annual Conference, which gives them the rights of voice and vote on all matters except the election of lay delegates to the General Conference.

Full Membership: When an adult member has completed the 90 day probationary period and their class leader feels that they are ready to be received into full membership, the pastor will read them into full membership which gives them voice and vote on all matters of the church.

G

General Board: The connectional administrative body of the African Methodist Episcopal Church who are responsible for supervising the financial program of all the church agencies that receive funds from the General Budget. Its actions are subject only to the General Conference and in the interim to the Judicial Council. The Episcopal District nominates them and the General Conference elects the members of the General Board every four years.

General Budget: The funds received from the local churches that give motion to the mission and ministries of the African Methodist Episcopal Church.

General Confession: The prayer of forgiveness recited by the celebrant and members of the congregation prior to celebrating the Lord's Supper.

General Officer: Persons elected by the General Conference for administrative functions. (*The Chief Financial Officer, Chief Information Officer, the Publisher, The Editor, The Executive Secretary of Christian Education, The Executive Secretary of the Department of Annuities Investments and Insurance, The Executive Director of the Department of Research and Scholarship, The Executive Director of Church Growth, The Executive Director of the Department of Global Witness*).

General Rules: A set of rules devised in 1738 by John Wesley for his societies. He did this to make clear the connection between the saving faith and Christian behavior and to indicate what was expected of persons, as they became members of the Methodist societies.

General Secretary: The highest-ranking staff officer and chief administrative staff person, charged with keeping an accurate account of all church proceedings.

Global Witness and Ministry Department: Formally called the Department of Missions. This is the missions' arm of the church that responds to the needs of people across the globe particularly during times of devastation. It is headquartered in Charleston, South Carolina.

Gloria in Excelsis Deo: (*Glory be to God on high*) the opening Latin words of the traditional hymn often sung as a part of the Sacrament of the Lord's Supper. *John 1:29.*

Gloria Patri: (*Glory be to the Father*). The opening Latin words for the widely used short hymn of praise to the Trinity. The familiar words are *Glory be to the Father, and to the Son, and to the Holy God; as it was in the beginning, is now, and ever shall be, world without end."* In our tradition it is sung following the Decalogue.

Good and Regular Standing: A qualification for holding any office or membership in the African Methodist Episcopal Church. They must regularly attend worship and the other means of grace; contribute regularly to the support of the gospel, the church, its benevolent enterprises, the poor; and to give one's time and talents to the various ministries of the church.

Good Friday: The Friday before Easter on which the crucifixion of Jesus is remembered. Good Friday services focus upon prayerful reflection on the death of Jesus Christ and penance and special devotion for the believer.

Gospel: From the Latin *evangelium,* meaning good tale or good news. The word is used in connection with the first four books of the New Testament: Matthew, Mark, Luke and John.

Grace: The unmerited favor bestowed upon believers in Jesus Christ.

H

Hallelujah: The highest praise that one can give to God.

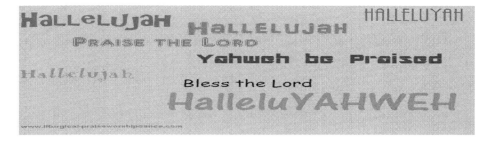

Heaven: The utopic place where believer's spirits are free from suffering in the afterlife.

Henotheism: Belief in a single Deity without denying the existence of others.

Holy Steward: A Historical term used to describe the member of the Steward Board who ensures that the elements for the sacrament of Holy Communion are available and that the sacristy is well stocked.

Holy Spirit: The third person of the Trinity. Often referred to as the Holy Ghost or the Paraclete.

Holy Thursday: The Thursday of Holy Week, the day on which the Last Supper and the institution of the Lord's Supper is commemorated. Since the Gospel of John records that the last supper included Jesus' washing of the disciples feet in some churches the ceremony of foot washing is observed on this day.

Holy Week: The week of Christian observances leading to Easter Sunday. It begins with Palm Sunday and progresses through Holy or Maundy Thursday and Good Friday. It culminated with the Easter Sunday celebration.

Horsemen The Four: *Richard Allen, Daniel Alexander Payne, William Paul Quinn and Henry McNeal Turner* greatly expanded, extended and enlarged the African Methodist Episcopal Church in its infancy.

Hosanna: An acclamation of praise and adoration to God. It comes from the Greek work *hosanna*, which serves as a translation for the Hebrew phrase meaning, *"save now, we pray."*

Hymn of Preparation: A hymn that is sung by the congregation prior to the Spoken Word during a Worship experience.

Hymn: Religious poems set to music that are sung during worship.

Hymnal: The African Methodist Episcopal Church Bicentennial Hymnal was published during the 1984-88 quadrennium. It has been updated and improved to include many modern hymns.

Lift up your voice - join the choir!

I

Immersion: One of the modes of baptism in which the candidate for baptism is placed in a pool and dunked under water as a demonstration for the remission of sins.

Intercession: Prayers or petitions on behalf of a person, a group of persons or general needs of the world. Prayers of intercession are an integral part of personal and congregational worship.

Initial Sermon: The phrase that refers to the presentation of a persons first preaching assignment. It has historically been referred to as a trial sermon.

Intinction: A method of partaking of the elements in the Sacrament of the Lord's Supper. In this procedure, the participant takes the bread and dips it into the wine in a large chalice held by the pastor. The participant then eats the moistened bread.

Invitation to Christian Discipleship: The invitation given by the pastor or another clergy person to those who would make a decision to declare their faith in Jesus Christ and join the church or both. Those who would make a decision are asked to come forward to the chancel railing.

Invocation: A prayer asking for a special sense of God's presence and guidance. It is typically offered following the hymn of praise during worship.

Itinerancy: The system in the African Methodist Episcopal Church by which ministers are appointed to their charges by the presiding bishop. The ministers are under obligation to serve where they are appointed for a one-year term, with a glad mind and a willing heart.

J

James Centre, F.C.: The operational headquarters of the 18th Episcopal District located in Maseru, Lesotho. It was constructed under the visionary leadership of Bishop Frederick Calhoun James in 1974. It is a model of self-help; it provides jobs, supports entrepreneurship and revenue for the ministry of the 18th district.

Jehovah: The Hebrew pronunciation of God.

Jesus: The sinless Son of God who was begotten and not made. He is the savior of the world.

Jones, Absalom: (1745-1818) was a follower of Richard Allen. He could not bear the indignity suffered at St. George's and therefore refused to become a member of another Methodist body so he joined St. Thomas Episcopal Church and was ordained as the first black priest in the Episcopal Church in America.

Judicial Council: The highest judicatory body of the African Methodist Episcopal Church. It is an Appellate Body (A *panel of review to determine whether or not the rulings and judgments of the subordinate panels are correct)* elected by the General Conference to which it is amenable.

Junior Board of Stewardesses: A board of members of the church who are in training to become members of the Senior Board of Stewardesses.

Junior Board of Stewards: A board of members of the church who are in training to become members of the Senior Board of Stewards.

Junior Board of Trustees: A board of members of the church who are in training to become members of the Senior Board of Trustees.

Jurisdiction: Limits or territory within which authority may be exercised specifically, the power to hear and determine a case.

Justification: A doctrinal belief that believers are received into Christ's presence without spot or blemish, just as we are.

K

Kwanzaa: The currency of the country of Angola. It is also the name used for a weeklong celebration in the United States December 26-31 meaning *"first fruits."*

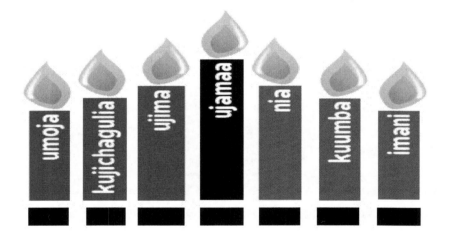

L

Laity: Taken form the Greek *Laos,* meaning, *"people."* In the Christian Church it has meant the people of God. More specifically laity designates those who are not ordained ministers.

Lay Electoral College: A body of laypersons elected from each station, circuit or mission in the Annual Conference whose purpose is to elect delegates to the General Conference in accordance with the Doctrine and Discipline of the African Methodist Episcopal Church.

Lay Organization: This entity of the African Methodist Episcopal Church includes any person who is not licensed or ordained to preach. They are the educational arm of the church. They offer instruction on the doctrine and discipline, history and polity of the church.

Lay Witness Sunday: A special Sunday established by the General Conference to be observed in every Episcopal District. It should be observed by having laypersons lead all parts of the worship and a lay speaker delivering the message.

Laying on of hands: The placing of hands on the head of an individual in various services to denote the conferring of the Holy Spirit. The laying on of hands is most common in services of baptism, confirmation, ordination and healing.

Lectern: A stand upon which the Bible is placed for reading in a worship service. The word lectern derives from the Latin word *legere*, which means to read.

Lectionary: This is a list or table of Scripture lessons or passages *(lections)* to be read in Sunday worship services or other specific occasions. The term *lectionary* is also used to refer to a book such as *The Common Lectionary,* which contains the listings or tables of passages.

Lent: A forty-day period of focus on penitence and preparation for the Resurrection Event of Easter. Lent begins on Ash Wednesday and ends at sunset on Easter Eve. The liturgical color for this season of the Christian year is Purple.

Letter of Withdrawal: Any member of the African Methodist Episcopal Church who is in good and regular standing may terminate their membership by submitting a letter of withdrawal to the pastor of the local congregation. The letter should be read at the Official Board and acted upon.

Licentiate: A person who has expressed a call to preach the gospel. They have preached an initial sermon before the local congregation, been examined, coached and counseled by the pastor, the steward board, the church conference and licensed by the quarterly conference, if they deem them to be fit.

Litany: A liturgical prayer consisting of a series of invocations and prayer requests. The litany usually consists of sections read alternately by the worship leader and the congregation.

Liturgical Colors: *White, Green, Purple, Violet, Royal Blue and Red.* Violet and royal blue are contemporary choices used as alternates to purple.

Liturgy: A prescribed form of ritual governing the words or actions for a ceremony, rite of body of rites, for public worship, more specifically referred to as Worship and Ritual in the Doctrine and Discipline of the African Methodist Episcopal Church.

Local Church: A congregation of believers who worship, study and pray together under the leadership of a duly appointed pastor.

Local Ministry: Those who are not itinerate ministers are local ministers. They function at the request and discretion of the local church and the local pastor.

Local: Relating to a specific place, a particular location of a branch.

Location of Clergy, administrative: Removal of an itinerate minister's right to practice ministry beyond the local church where their membership is located. Administrative location is exercised for those ministers who have been unable to perform effectively or competently the duties of the itinerate ministry. These located ministers are limited in the exercise of their ministerial rights to the local church in which they have their membership, only. *Administrative location* is voted by the lay and clergy delegates within an annual conference upon recommendation by the Ministerial Efficiency Committee.

Location of Clergy, honorable: The process by which a minister may request to be relieved of the requirement to *"travel"* or to be a part of the itinerate ministry of the African Methodist Episcopal Church. Honorable location is granted to ministers who are in good standing in the Annual Conference. A located minister may exercise ministerial functions only in the local church where their membership is held. Whether or not to award the status of honorable location is voted on by the members of the Annual Conference upon the recommendation of the Ministerial Efficiency Committee.

Location of Clergy: The process by which the authority of a clergy person to exercise the rights and privileges of a minister throughout the denomination are withdrawn. A located minister retains the right to exercise ministerial rights only within the local church in which their membership is held. The word *location* has a particular meaning in the context of Methodism in the United States. Historically, when a person was judged by the Annual Conference to have gifts and graces to serve effectively as a minister throughout the denomination, that person became a *"traveling elder."* A traveling elder is one who is considered qualified to serve wherever appointed and thus to become a part of the itinerate or traveling ministry. When a minister is no longer able, willing or judged competent to travel throughout the church, the privilege of traveling should be withdrawn and the minister is located, (*that is limited to only one place*). The use of the word *location* in the denomination today is based upon this historical usage.

Lord's Prayer, the: The name generally given to the prayer found in Matthew 6:9-13 and in a shorter form in Luke 11:2-4. It is widely used in services of worship and is an important part of the ritual for the Sacrament of the Lord's Supper.

Lord's Supper, the: Commonly called the Eucharist, or Communion. It is one of two sacraments celebrated by the elder in the local church on festive days as well as the first Sunday of each month.

Lord's Table, the: Another term in the African Methodist Episcopal Church for the communion table.

Love Feast: The service of preparation, which preceded the sacrament of the Lord's Supper. The elements for the love feast are water, symbolic of our desire for purification and bread symbolic of our desire for goodwill with one another. In this service of forgiveness the believer receives grace from Jesus Christ and extends forgiveness to their brothers and sisters in Christ, which makes us acceptable before the Lord at the Holy Table.

M

Maladministration: A charge that can be levied against a clergy person who is believed to be in violation of the administrative duties of their office as outlined in the Doctrine and Discipline.

Manse: A term used to describe the living quarters owned by the denomination held in trust by the local trustees where the pastor resides while serving that congregation.

Maundy Thursday: *See Holy Thursday*

McKenzie-Murphy, Vashti: The former pastor of Payne Memorial AME Church in Baltimore, Maryland who was the first elected and consecrated female Bishop of the African Methodist Episcopal Church in the year 2000. The General Conference met in Cincinnati, Ohio.

Meet: Precisely adapted to a particular situation, need or circumstance as stated in the Catechism of Faith, question 3.

Member: A person who has been baptized and enters into the covenant of being received into fellowship of the church as provided by the Doctrine and Discipline of the African Methodist Episcopal Church.

Membership Roll: The permanent record of the membership of the local African Methodist Episcopal Church. The membership roll included the names, addresses, date of birth and date of baptism of all persons who have come into membership by confession of faith, or by transfer.

Mid Year Convocation: A mid year meeting of all of the churches in an episcopal district held at the call of the bishop where the presiding elders report one half of the budget requests.

Minister of Music: The title given to the person who is in charge of the total music program in the local church.

Ministerial Efficiency Committee: An Annual Conference Committee appointed by the presiding bishop to review the efficiency and moral conduct of those ministers who are referred to it.

Ministerial Tools: In our tradition candidates for ordination are required to always carry the following tools with them: *a Bible, a Discipline and an AME Hymnal.*

Mission: A small congregation that has very few members is often referred to as a mission.

Missionary Rule: A term used when a person is serving as the pastor of a church without the proper educational or time credentials. This is only at the discretion of the presiding bishop.

Missionary: One who goes into the highways and hedges to lift those who are on the fridges of society, the poor, the sick and the indigent.

Monotheism: The belief that there is only one God.

Mother Bethel: Is the first congregation in the denominations history. It is located at Sixth and Lombard Streets in Philadelphia, Pennsylvania. It sits on the oldest continuously piece of property owned by African Americans.

Mother Church West of the Mississippi River: St. Paul Church in St. Louis, Missouri is the mother church west of the Mississippi it was founded in1841.

Motto: The motto of the African Methodist Episcopal Church is: God our Father, Humankind our Family, and The Holy Spirit our Comforter.

MSWAWO plus P.K.'s: Minister Spouses Widows and Widower Organization plus Preachers Kids. It is the official clergy family organization of the African Methodist Episcopal Church.

N

N.G.O.: Non-Governmental Organization. The United Nations, headquartered in New York City bestowed NGO status the Women's Missionary Society of the African Methodist Episcopal Church.

Narthex: That portion of a church building between the outside door or other portion of the building and the entrance door of the sanctuary.

National Council of Churches of Christ in the U.S.A. (NCCC): The chief ecumenical organization of the Anglican, Catholic, Orthodox and Protestant denominations, which provided services and speaks to important issues. Bishop Philip Robert Cousin is a former president of this organization.

Nave: The main section of the sanctuary of a church building in which the congregation is seated during the worship service. The nave is the area located between the main entrance from the outside of the narthex to the chancel area or railing.

New Member: The membership status of a person joining the African Methodist Episcopal Church who comes from no previous faith tradition.

New Member's Class: A class that is taught to persons who join the church to enlighten them to the history and polity of the church.

New Testament: A collection of biblical writings that depict the life and ministry of Jesus. They range from Matthew to Revelation. It includes twenty-seven books.

Nicene Creed: Frequently used as an affirmation of faith by Christians. The Nicene Creed is the historic statement of belief of the Christian faith devised by the Council of Nicea in 325 A.D. The Council of Constantinople revised the creed in 381 A.D. It is the second oldest creed of faith.

Nichols, Decatur Ward: (1900-2004) A bishop in the African Methodist Episcopal Church who migrated from Charleston, South Carolina to New York City and was the popular pastor of Emanuel AME Church in New York, City, which grew to more than 3,000 between 1925 and 1940. In 1940 at the age of 39 he was elected the 59th bishop of the African Methodist Episcopal Church. He is often referred to as *Poppa Nic.*

Nominated: To formally enter as a candidate for election for an honor or award. In the church the pastor nominates the Stewards, they are then confirmed by the quarterly conference. The pastor nominates trustees, however the members of the church conference elect them.

O

Oblation: The act of offering something in religious worship. In the African Methodist Episcopal Church, it is Christ the perfect one offering to God for sinful humanity.

Offering: The gifts and tithes brought by worshipers to the service for the support of the ministry.

Offertory: The musical selection sung or played while the tithes and offerings are being received from the members of the congregation.

Official Board: The gathering of all of the leaders in a congregation every week or month to transact the business of the local church.

Officiant: The clergy person who presides during a funeral service or at the solemnization of matrimony.

Old Testament: The thirty-nine books of the pre-Christian era considered authoritative and canonical by most Protestant churches.

Order of Worship: The progression of the worship celebration in the African Methodist Episcopal Church. It begins with a prelude and ends with the benediction.

Ordination: The act of conferring ministerial orders. A bishop performs ordination(s). The central portion of the ceremony are the words granting the authority of the order of deacon or elder and the laying on of hands by the bishop and others on the person being ordained.

Orthodox: An adhering to the accepted or traditional and established faith.

Overseas Districts: Typically referring to districts 14-20.

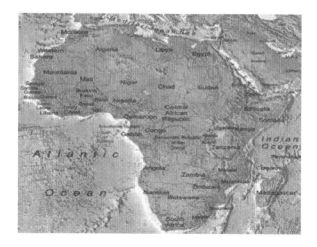

P

Pall: The cloth covering placed over a casket during a funeral. When a pall is used, flowers are not placed on the casket.

Pallbearers: Those persons who carry the casket in the course of a funeral. In some funerals, additional persons who do not carry the casket are called honorary pallbearers.

Palm Sunday (Passion Sunday): The Sunday immediately proceeding Easter Sunday. Palm Sunday commemorates the entry of Jesus into Jerusalem and begins the series of observances focusing on the events of Holy Week. This Sunday is also often referred to as Passion Sunday, marking the beginning of the passion or suffering of Jesus leading to and including the crucifixion.

Palms: The leaves of the palm tree used in many churches as part of the procession and the observances of the Palm Sunday worship services. The palms symbolize the response of the people to the entry of Jesus into Jerusalem at the beginning of Holy Week. They are burned before the following Ash Wednesday; their remains become the ashes.

Paraments: The linens and cloth hangings used on communion tables, altars, pulpits and lecterns. The colors of the paraments reflect the traditional colors of the seasons of the Christian year. The paraments are changed as the seasons of the Christian year progress. Often the paraments are embellished with specific symbols appropriate to the Christian season. In many churches, stewardesses, the altar guild or lay volunteers are responsible for the care and changing of the paraments.

Parsonage: Housing provided for or owned by the congregation where the pastor and their family reside while serving a given congregation.

Pastor: An ordained or licensed person who is the spiritual leader appointed by the presiding bishop or presiding elder as the official leader of a local station, circuit or mission who is responsible for the total program of the church to which they are appointed.

Pastor's Annual Report: The report that is prepared by the pastor. It is signed by the pastor and the elected delegate. It is read on the floor of the Annual Conference. Only those items that the Bishops desires to hear are read.

Pastor's Package: The term used to describe the negotiated compensation of the local pastor.

Pastor's Steward: A historical phrase, which denotes the member of a local churches steward board who takes special care to supply or cause the pastor's need to be met.

Pastoral Care: The act of a pastor assisting members of their congregation or community with counseling, prayer, advice or any spiritual need the person may have.

Payne Theological Seminary: The only free standing predominantly African American Seminary in the world, founded in 1844 incorporated in 1891, located in Wilberforce, Ohio. It is a leader in on-line theological education.

Payne, Daniel Alexander: (1811-1893) The Apostle of Education in the African Methodist Episcopal Church. He purchased Wilberforce University from the Methodist Episcopal Church, South in 1856 for $10,000. He served simultaneously as a Bishop in the church and the President of Wilberforce University. Payne Theological Seminary is also named in his honor.

Peace, the: The ancient and traditional practice of Christians greeting one another with a sign or word of love and blessing. This is done with an embrace, a handshake, a handclasp, or the exchange of a word of blessing.

Pentecost: One of the principal days of the Christian year, celebrated on the fiftieth day after Easter. The Greek word *pentecoste* means "fiftieth day." Pentecost is the day on which the Christian Church commemorates the coming of the Holy Spirit upon the Apostles and others assembled in Jerusalem. It marks the beginning of the Christian Church and the proclamation of its message throughout the world and is often referred to as the birthday of the church. The liturgical color for Pentecost is red.

Perfection: The state or condition of being perfect. The believer continually strives for perfection. However, it is only attained in eternal life.

Periodicals: The African Methodist Episcopal Church offers the following periodicals: *The Christian Recorder, The AME Review, The Voice of Missions, The Missionary Magazine, The Journal Of Christian Education, The Secret Chamber and The Y. P.D. Newsletter.*

Petition: In the broadest sense, an earnest request, prayer, or supplication to God. Often such petitions are intercessory prayers, lifting the concerns for an individual or a group to God.

Pew: A long bench used for the seating of worshipers in churches. The current usage of the word *pew* derives from the enclosed space or compartment in a church in which benches or seats were provided for a family and for which a pewage or pew rental was required.

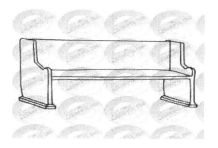

Piety: Is a virtue that means religious devotion, spirituality or a combination of both.

Polemic: A disputation unit that intends to degrade or attack an idea or subject, as illustrated in the tower of Babel.

Polity: A society or institution with an organized form of government; a specific form of church government.

Post Conference Convocation (*Planning Meeting*): Following the series of Annual Conference in an episcopal district the bishop holds a post conference convocation to set the program for the ensuing conference year.

Prayer desk, prayer bench, or prie-Dieu: A small kneeling bench designed to be used by a person at prayer. The prie-Dieu (*which in French means literally "pray God"*) is often built with a raised shelf on which the elbows or a book may be placed.

Prayer of Consecration: The prayer recited by the celebrant during the sacrament of Holy Communion.

Prayer of Humiliation: One of the prayers recited by the Elder during the celebration of the sacrament of Holy Communion.

Pre-exile: The period in Biblical History before the Babylonian exile.

Prelude: The musical selection played or sung at the beginning of a worship service. It is generally considered a part of the gathering time for congregations.

Preparatory Member: Refers to children who have been baptized and are under the age of 12. The pastor and congregation should be preparing them to become full members.

President of the Bishops Council: An active Bishop serves as the President of the Bishop's Council in the order of their election for the term of one year from June 15 to June 15 of the following year.

President of the General Board: An Active Bishop serves as the President of the General Board for a term of two years.

Presiding Elder: A middle manager that is appointed by the presiding bishop to supervise a geographical area within the annual conference. They are required to visit all of the churches quarterly to assess the spiritual and fiscal affairs of the congregation and make recommendations to the Bishop.

Presiding Elder's Council: There is a connectional and an episcopal district council of presiding elder's. All presiding elders are members. They meet to discuss issues germain to their position.

Primus Inter Pares: A Latin term which means *First Among Equals*. It is used when referring to the Bishops of the church.

Propitiation: A Greek word meaning *living sacrifice.* Jesus was our propitiation.

Proselyte: A person who is persuaded to convert to another religion.

Pro-Tem: A historical term in the African Methodist Episcopal Church. It originates from the Greek term, which means *temporary chair.* Some pastors appoint pro-tems to act as vice chair persons of the board of stewards and trustees, however we errantly use the term since its meaning is temporary, any member of the board can serve as the pro-tem because this is not a permanent position.

Psalter: A separate book or portion of a book or hymnal containing the Psalms. The psalter often contains the Psalms arranged for singing or liturgical or developmental use.

Public Offering: At most worship experiences in the African Methodist Episcopal Church, there will be a public offering for the continuation of the work of the kingdom.

Publishing House: The African Methodist Episcopal Church owns and operates our own publishing house located at 500 Eighth Avenue, South in Nashville, Tennessee.

Pulpit: A stand or tall reading desk used by the minister for preaching or for conducting a service of worship. In most Churches the pulpit sits on a raised dais.

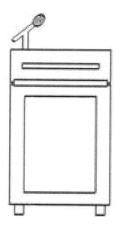

Q

Quadrennium: A period of four years. The General Conference meets only once every four years. Officially the four-year quadrennium begins on January 1 following the adjournment of the General Conference.

Quarterly Conference: One of the five conferences in the African Methodist Episcopal Church, that meets four times per year. The Presiding Elder visits each pastoral charge to examine the spiritual, fiscal and emotional health of a congregation and receives reports from the various auxiliaries of the local church.

Quorum: A quorum is a majority of those persons who are eligible to vote. At a duly called meeting those present constitute a quorum.

R

Reobligation: The act of binding one to affirm certain vows. Typically used when changing the status of one from another denomination or from a local to an itinerate minister.

Report Meeting: A meeting called by the Presiding Elder in which each pastor is responsible for reporting a portion of his or her congregation's budgetary obligations.

Resident Bishop: A Methodist term referring to a presiding bishop who is living within the confines of their respective episcopal district.

Responsive Reading: Readings during a worship celebration that are read responsively by the leader and the congregation.

Retreat: A period of time spent away from the regular routine. A retreat is often used for study and spiritual growth, either by an individual or by members of a group.

Reverend, The: The accepted ascription of respect in English for a clergy person. When the ascription is written, the word *Reverend* is an adjective and must be followed by the noun modified. Therefore, the definite article *The* should always precede the word *Reverend,* which is then followed by the appropriate title and name, such as The Reverend Mr. Smith or The Reverend John Smith.

Revisions Committee: A committee of the General Conference with the responsible for sifting through the proposed legislation prior to the General Conference and recommending only those pieces of proposed legislation that they think are worthy of consideration by the body.

Richard Allen Young Adult Council: A networking organization in the African Methodist Episcopal Church for those persons between 21 and 39 years of age. They teach discipleship, leadership training and enjoy fellowship.

Ritual: A specific form including text for the conducting of a service. Usually, the ritual has been established by custom and tradition.

Rolls, Membership: Those records that each local church is required to maintain on the membership. The various membership rolls are:

1. Full Membership Roll

2. Prepartory Membership Roll

3. Affiliate Membership Roll

4. Active Membership Roll

5. Annual Conference Membership Roll

Rubrics: The directions or rules given for the proper conduct of worship rituals and services. The word *rubric comes* form the Latin word for red.

Rules, General: A set of directions for Christian behavior espousing the genuine and sincere quest for salvation which may be achieved through the refraining from evil, engaging in good works and availing one's self of all of the ordinances of God. John Wesley authored these General Rules of the United Societies.

S

Sacrament: A religious ceremony considered especially sacred because of God's acting through the sacrament or because it is a sign or symbol of a significant reality.

S.A.D.A.: The Service and Development Agency of the African Methodist Episcopal Church. This is the agency that responds to natural disasters, in addition to development in the Caribbean and Africa. There have been two chairpersons in its history Bishop Donald G.K. Ming and the current chair, Bishop Mc Kinley Young.

Sacristy: The room generally located immediately at the front of the church sanctuary, often just off the chancel area, where the paraments, communion ware and other materials for the communion table and chancel are kept.

Saint George's Church: The Methodist Episcopal Church in Philadelphia, Pennsylvania where Richard Allen and his cohorts were pulled from their knees while they were praying.

Sanctification: The state of growing in divine grace as a result of a Christian commitment after baptism or conversion.

Sanctuary: The main worship room or auditorium in an African Methodist Episcopal Church building.

Sanctus: An ancient hymn of adoration beginning with the words, "*Holy, holy, holy,*" and used as a part of the Sacrament of the Lord's Supper. Sanctus is the Latin word for holy.

Scripture Lesson: A designated passage of the Bible read in the course of a worship celebration. Often African Methodist Episcopal worship services include a Scripture lesson or reading from the Old Testament and from the New Testament Gospels or Epistles or both.

Secretary of the Church: The phrase used to refer to the General Secretary of the African Methodist Episcopal Church.

Secretary, Annual Conference: The person elected to be responsible for the proper development and maintenance of the records of the Annual Conference. The secretary of the Annual Conference is responsible for maintaining the official record of the daily proceedings or minutes of the Annual Conference sessions, compiling and publishing the minutes and keeping records pertaining to ministerial trials, records of official certificates and credentials and other specific documents and records. The secretary is elected by the Annual Conference and is usually an ordained itinerate elder.

Seminary: The African Methodist Episcopal Church owns and operates two Theological Seminaries in the United States: Payne, located in Wilberforce, Ohio and Turner, located in Atlanta, Georgia.

Senior Bishop: A presiding bishop who is first in seniority. It is purely a ceremonial designation, although they preside first at connectional public worship celebrations.

Senior Episcopal Supervisor: The spouse of the Senior Bishop. This is also a purely ceremonial designation.

Senior Pastor: An unofficial term used to describe the pastor of a local congregation. Our polity only permits one pastor at each charge.

Septuagint: The Greek translation of the Jewish scriptures dating to the 3rd century B.C.E. It's name *(from Latin, "seventy")* is derived from the legend that 72 scholars did the work of translation in 72 days.

Servant Leadership: A philosophy and set of practices that enriches the lives of individuals and builds better communities and churches.

Servant: A person in the service of or for the benefit of others.

Sexual Harassment: Any unwelcomed, unsolicited touching, comments or gestures of a sexual nature.

Shaffer, Bishop C.T.: Was a fair skinned person who was elected and consecrated the 29th bishop of the church at the General Conference of 1900, chiefly because Bishop Abraham Grant took up the cry *"we must elect one of our white Negros' a bishop."*

Simony: The act of paying to receive sacraments including those for ordination to a holy office or other position of a religious nature *(i.e. an appointment)*.

Sine Die: A term used to close a session of an Annual Conference, which means adjournment with no fixed day for a future meeting.

Social Action: An organized program of socioeconomic reform with a grassroots foundation.

Social Holiness: An awareness of and sensitivity to the social needs of a society.

Society: An organized group working together or periodically meeting because of common interests, beliefs, or concerns. Generally referred to, in our usage as a local congregation.

Sons of Allen: The Men's Ministry of the African Methodist Episcopal Church. This ministry is composed of three or more men formed for the purpose of encouraging men to become involved in helping other men find Christ in their lives. They have a designated uniform: *burgundy blazer, white shirt, burgundy tie and grey slacks.*

Spiritual Formation: The growth and development of the whole person by an internal focus.

Station: A pastoral charge comprising only one local church. This is in contrast to a circuit, which contains two or more local churches.

Steward Board: A board of persons appointed by the pastor annually to serve as spiritual advisors to the pastor and the congregation. They are nominated by the pastor and confirmed by the quarterly conference. There must be a minimum of three and a maximum of nineteen persons serving on this board.

Steward: A person of solid piety who both knows and loves the African Methodist doctrine and discipline. These officers are appointed by the pastor for a term of one year and confirmed by the quarterly conference.

Stewardess: Women who assist the stewards in their duties. They take particular care of the altar and preparation for Holy Communion. Their dress code is a long white dress with and a white dooly or cap on their head.

Stewardship Finance Commission: A commission in the local church that is charged with the responsibility of taking an accurate account of all funds received and expended. There should by law of the church be three stewards, three trustees and three at large members of this commission.

Stewardship: Exercising and engaging in the activity of caring for what one has been placed in charge of.

Stewardship: The practice of systematically and proportionate giving of time, influence, ability and material possession based on the conviction that these are a trust from God.

Stole: A long narrow strip of material worn by ordained and diaconal ministers. Deacons and diaconal ministers by custom wear the stole over the left shoulder only. Ordained elders, including bishops wear the stole around the neck over both shoulders. The stole worn in a service of worship is usually of the appropriate color for the day or season of the Christian calendar.

Sunbeam: A term used to describe children in the church who are 5-9 years of age.

Superannuated Preacher(s): A term applied to an ordained itinerate elder who retires from the active ministry because of age or disability.

Supernumerary Preacher(s): A term applied to an ordained itinerate elder for whom there is no appointment available or one who is allowed to be without appointment at their request.

Supply Pastor: A clergy person, usually a local deacon, elder, licentiate or itinerate deacon who is not in full connection who is serving a congregation at the request of the presiding elder.

Surplice: A loose white vestment with large open sleeves that generally extends to the knees in length. The surplice is usually worn as an outer garment over a cassock. Acolytes, choir members and some clergy persons sometimes wear it in African Methodist Episcopal worship celebrations.

Surrender of Credentials: The procedure whereby a local deacon, elder or an itinerate deacon or elder return their credentials upon leaving the ministry of the African Methodist Episcopal Church. When they leave the connection and withdraw, they must surrender their credentials given to them by the Annual Conference. The credentials are to be surrendered to the presiding elder and deposited with the Conference Secretary.

Sustentation: The act of sustaining or being sustained; its usages by the church primarily referred to providing meals/lodging and or expenses of a member, delegate or representative at scheduled meetings, conventions or conferences.

T

Te Deum, Ladamus: A Latin term meaning
We Praise you, O God.

Termination of Local Church Membership (lay): The
membership of any layperson in the African Methodist
Episcopal Church may be terminated by: *Death,
Expulsion or by request of the member.*

Testify, Testimony: The act of giving an account of or
witnessing to one's faith in a public setting such as a
prayer meeting, study group, or a worship service.
Testimony is used to refer to the content of what is said
or written by the person testifying.

The Lord's Supper or Holy Communion: The Sacrament instituted by Jesus Christ when he celebrated the Last Supper with his disciples, consisting of bread and wine representing His body and blood as a sacrifice for the forgiveness of sins. It is commonly observed among us on the first Sunday of each month and other special festive days.

Theophany: A manifestation of God to humans through an appearance, such as an angel or some natural phenomenon.

Tithing: A biblical mandate governing the individual's support (10% of ones total income) of the mission and ministry of the church symbolizing one's commitment to Christ and his church.

Weekly Pledge Guidelines				
Weekly Income	10%	5%	4%	2%
$200	$20	$10	$8	$4
$500	$50	$25	$20	$10
$750	$75	$37	$30	$15
$1,000	$100	$50	$40	$20
$1,500	$150	$75	$60	$30
$2,000	$200	$100	$80	$40

Transfer of a Clergyperson: An ordained itinerate elder who is in good and regular standing in an Annual Conference has the right to request a transfer to any annual conference or episcopal district in the connection.

Transfer of Membership: Any member of the local church who is in good and regular standing has the right to transfer their membership to any African Methodist Episcopal Church in the connection.

Transfer of Property: Trustees hold all real and personal property in trust for the connectional church. No property can be legally transferred without the expressed written consent of the trustee board of the local, conference or connectional level.

Transubstantiation: The doctrinal belief that during the consecration of the Eucharist/Holy Communion the physical presence of the bread and wine are transformed into the actual body and blood of Christ.

Treasurer/Chief Financial Officer: Is elected every four years at the site of the General Conference and is responsible to fulfill the mandates as outlined in the connectional budget. The treasurer maintains office space in Nashville, Tennessee and Washington, D.C.

Trifling: Lacking in significant or solid worth, culturally or substantively refers to laziness or wasting time.

Trust Clause in deeds: The clause that must be included in the deeds of all African Methodist Episcopal Church properties. The local church in trust for the denomination holds all property.

Trustee Training: The discipline requires that every person who is elected to serve as a member of the Trustee Board must be trained annually of their duties and responsibilities.

Trustee: Persons nominated by the pastor and elected annually by members of the congregation to manage the temporal concerns of the church. They are accountable to the quarterly conference. They hold all real and personal property in trust for the connection.

Turner Henry, McNeal: The 12th bishop of the African Methodist Episcopal Church, who was elected to the Georgia State House of Representatives and was the first African American Chaplain to serve in the United States Army. President Abraham Lincoln appointed him.

Turner Theological Seminary: A seminary founded in 1894, owned and operated by the African Methodist Episcopal Church located in Atlanta, Georgia and it is a part of the Interdenominational Theological Center.

U

Unauthorized Assessments: It is illegal for any person clergy or lay representing the African Methodist Episcopal Church to request or receive any assessments other than those authorized by the General Conference.

Unorthodox: A term referring to something that is not orthodox.

Usher: A person who guards the entry doors to the sanctuary.

U S H E R S

V

Versicle: A short verse or sentence said or sung by a minister or worship leader and immediately followed with a response by the congregation. A choir and a congregation, two halves of a choir or by a minister and a choir also use versicles.

Vesper Service: A late afternoon or early evening worship service.

Vestibule: The hallway outside the doors that enter into the sanctuary.

Vestments: Items of clothing such as robes, gowns, or other special garments and stoles worn by ministers and lay persons while conducting worship services.

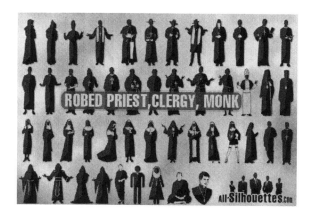

Vigil: A service or period of prayers and devotions held on the night before or in the early morning of important religious days or festivals. On occasion special vigils are organized around a specific concern or issue in a local church. The word vigil comes from the Latin *vigil,* meaning to watch.

Virgin: A woman who has not had sexual intercourse with a man. Usually referring to the Virgin Mary, the earthly vessel that bore Jesus into this world.

W

Wafer: The thin, circular disk of unleavened bread used in the Sacrament of the Lord's Supper.

gg60887526 www.gograph.com

Walker, Taylor Yvonne: (1916-2010) a college educator, the daughter of Bishop Dougal Ormonde Beaconsfield Walker. The first female president of Wilberforce University 1984-1988.

Walking With the Bishop: A term that refers to an ordained itinerate clergy person who is being reassigned to another congregation. They walk with the bishop through the series of Annual Conferences until the bishop finds an appropriate assignment. In some cases the episcopal district will compensate the pastor until they are assigned.

Watch Night Service: A worship celebration mandated by the Doctrine and Discipline the African Methodist Episcopal Church, it is to be held on. December 31st of each year beginning at 10:30 p.m. and lasting until midnight.

Wedding Ring: The ring or band given by the groom to the bride in the Service of Christian Marriage as a symbol of the wedding vows taken. In recent years it has become quite common for the bride to also give a ring to the groom.

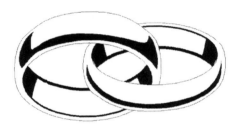

Wesley Charles: (1707-1788) the brother of John Wesley. He was an English hymn writer who wrote over 5500 hymns.

Wesley Quadrilateral, the: The phrase which has recently come into use to describe the principal factors that John Wesley believed illuminated the core of the Christian faith for the believer. Wesley did not formulate the succinct statement now commonly called the Wesley Quadrilateral. Building on the Anglican theological tradition, Wesley added a forth emphasis, experience. The resulting four components or "sides" of the quadrilateral are *(1) Scripture, (2) tradition, (3) reason, and (4) experience.* For African Methodist Episcopalians, Experience is considered the primary source and standard for Christian doctrine.

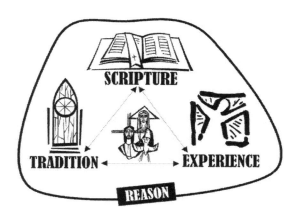

Wesley, John: The founder of the Methodist movement. He was born in 1703 in Epworth, England. He was a prolific preacher and writer and his writings provided a core of standard doctrine and interpretation to guide the new Methodist movement. In 1784, he sent instructions to America for the formation of a separate Methodist Church for the United States.

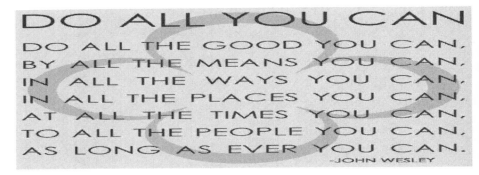

DO ALL YOU CAN

DO ALL THE GOOD YOU CAN,
BY ALL THE MEANS YOU CAN,
IN ALL THE WAYS YOU CAN,
IN ALL THE PLACES YOU CAN,
AT ALL THE TIMES YOU CAN,
TO ALL THE PEOPLE YOU CAN,
AS LONG AS EVER YOU CAN.
—JOHN WESLEY

Wine: The traditional term used by most Christians for the element used in the Sacrament of the Lord's Supper. The wine in the sacrament symbolizes the blood of Christ, which was shed for the redemption of all persons.

Withdrawal of Membership, Ministerial: The action on the part of the ministerial member of the African Methodist Episcopal Church. A minister may withdraw in order to join another denomination. However, they are required to surrender their ministerial credentials *(ordination papers)* to the presiding elder and or the annual conference secretary.

Women in Ministry (W.I.M.): A connectional organization for women in ministry within the African Methodist Episcopal Church. They meet to foster spiritual growth and communication between its members.

Women's Missionary Society (W.M.S.): Founded in 1944 in Philadelphia, Pennsylvania, it is a global organization, which develops and implements mission projects around the globe in the name of the African Methodist Episcopal Church. They convene an Executive Board meeting each year in January and a quadrennial meeting every four years. Their office headquarters are located in Washington, D.C. The precursors of the W.M.S. are the Women's Parent Mite, founded in May 1874 and the Women Home of Foreign Mission founded in 1893.

Works of Supererogation: Voluntary works, besides, over and above God's Commandments, which they call works of supererogation.

World Communion Sunday: One of the special Sundays during the Christian year, usually on the first Sunday in October.

World Council of Churches: A worldwide association of Christian churches. The African Methodist Episcopal Church is a member. Its headquarters is located in Geneva, Switzerland. Bishop Vinton Randolph Anderson served has the President of the North American branch of the WCC.

World Methodist Council: An organization comprising churches throughout the world that share a Wesleyan or Methodist heritage. Its headquarters is located in Lake Junaluska, North Carolina. Bishop Sarah Frances Taylor Davis, the 126th elected and consecrated bishop of the African Methodist Episcopal Church served as the Vice President.

Worship, The Book of: Contains resources to assist African Methodist Episcopal ministers and other worship leaders in directing and facilitating the worship experiences in the local churches.

Y

Yahweh: The Hebrew pronunciation for God.

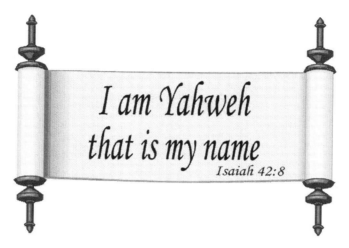

I am Yahweh that is my name
Isaiah 42:8

Yellow Fever Epidemic: Of 1793 in Philadelphia, Pennsylvania, 5,000 people were listed in the official register as having the deadly disease. Richard Allen and the Free African Society provided assistance to those families who were affected by this epidemic.

Young adults: Those persons who are out of high school and eighteen through thirty years of age. This definition of young adults is used in the African Methodist Episcopal Church as the basis for program development and implementation and for the meeting the requirements for determining representatives to various organizations.

Young People's Department: Is the organism where under the auspices of the Christian Education Department and the Women's Missionary Society that our young people are taught how to become model Christian citizens.

Young Women's Initiative: Those young ladies who are between the ages of eighteen and forty, who are members of the Women's Missionary Society. This ministry is designed to give this group a voice in the organization.

Youth: Those persons from approximately twelve through seventeen years of age. This definition of youth is used in the African Methodist Episcopal Church as the basis for program development and implementation and for meeting the representational requirements.

Z

Zenith: An Arabic expression meaning *"direction of the head."*

Zion: A Hebrew term used for a synonym of Jerusalem.

ACRONYMS AND ABBREVIATIONS USED

IN THE

AFRICAN METHODIST EPISCOPAL CHURCH

A

AA	Administrative Aide
ABS	American Bible Society
AC	Annual Conference
ACCT	Accountant
ACEL	Allen Christian Endeavor League
AMEC	The African Methodist Episcopal Church
AMEZ	The African Methodist Episcopal Zion Church

B

BOE	Board of Examiners
BOS	Board of Stewards
BOT	Board of Trustees
BS	Bishop

C

CED	Christian Education Department
CEF	Christian Educators Fellowship
CFO	Chief Financial Officer
CIO	Chief Information Officer
CMEC	The Christian Methodist Episcopal Church
CO	Connectional Officer
COB	Council of Bishops
COCU	Consultation of Church Union
CWS	Church World Service

D

DC	District Conference
DEA	Deacon
DOLA	Director of Lay Activities

E

ELD	Elder

F

FM   Full Member

FMC   The Free Methodist Church

G

GB   General Board

GC   General Conference

GCC   General Conference Commission

GDC   Global Development Council

GO   General Officer

GS   General Secretary

H

I

ITC   Interdenominational Theological Center

J

JC   Judicial Council

K

L

LD	Local Deacon
LE	Local Elder
LL	Lay Leader
LIC	Licentiate
LOC	Located
LP	Local Pastor

M

MC	Methodist Church
MEC	Methodist Episcopal Church
MEC	Ministerial Efficiency Committee
MEF	Ministerial Education Fund
MPC	Methodist Protestant Church

N

| NCCC | National Council of Churches of Christ in the U.S.A. |

O

| OM | Ordained Minister |

P

PE	Presiding Elder
PH	Publishing House
PM	Probationary Member
PME	Promotion and Missionary Education
PR	Pastor
PRM	Preparatory Member
PTS	Payne Theological Seminary
PUB	Publisher

Q

QC	Quarterly Conference
QCR	Quarterly Conference Report

R

RAYAC	Richard Allen Young Adult Council
RET	Retired

S

SOA	Sons of Allen
SR	Senior
SUPV	Supervisor

T

U

UMC   The United Methodist Church

V

W

WCC   World Council of Churches

WMC   World Methodist Council

WMS   Women's Missionary Society

WIM   Women In Ministry

X

Y

YAR   Young Adult Representative

YPD   Young People's Department

YWI   Young Women's Initiative

Z

REFERENCED MATERIALS FOR

ADDITONAL READING

Handbook of the Christian Year, Hoyt L. Hickman, Don E. Saliers, Lawrence Hull Stookey and James F. White. (Nashville: Abingdon Press, 1986).

The African Methodist Episcopal Church: Know Your Church Manual, Andrew White. (Nashville: The African Methodist Episcopal Church Publishing House, 1965).

The Bicentennial Hymnal of the African Methodist Episcopal Church. (Nashville: The African Methodist Episcopal Church, Publishing House, 1984).

*The Book of Discipline of the African Methodist Episcopal Church. (*Nashville: The African Methodist Episcopal Church, Publishing House, 2013).

The Encyclopedia of World Methodism, vols. 3 and 4, Nolan B. Harmon, general ed. (Nashville: The United Methodist Publishing House, 2004).

The Genius and Theory of Methodist Polity, Bishop Henry McNeal Turner. (Nashville: The African Methodist Episcopal Church Publishing House, 1986).

Preface to the History of the A.M.E. Church, Bishop Reverndy Cassius Ransom. (Nashville: The African Methodist Episcopal Church Publishing House, 1989).

ABOUT THE AUTHOR

Dr. Eric L. Brown was born in Johnstown, Pennsylvania. He received his formal education in the Johnstown Public School system and graduated from Greater Johnstown Senior High School. He matriculated at Wilberforce University, where he earned a Bachelor of Arts degree in Psychology and Religion and the Master of Divinity degree with a concentration in Homiletics from Payne Theological Seminary under the tutelage of Bishop Richard Allen Hildebrand and Dr. Louis-Charles Harvey. He earned a Doctor of Ministry degree from Ashland Theological Seminary. His dissertation is entitled *"A Paradigm for Lay Ministry."* He has served as a Visiting Lecturer at Pittsburgh Theological Seminary as well as visiting lecturer and keynote preacher at the German National Baptist Convention.

He professed Jesus Christ as his Lord and Savior at an early age and acknowledged his call to preach at the tender at of 17. He was subsequently licensed to preach the Gospel by the Presiding Elder Paul P. Martin at Bethel African Methodist Episcopal Church in Johnstown, Pennsylvania. He was ordained as an Itinerate Deacon by Bishop Richard Allen Hildebrand and an Elder by Bishop Henry Allen Belin in the Pittsburgh Annual Conference of the African Methodist Episcopal Church.

He pastored churches in Ohio prior to being transferred to the Pittsburgh Annual Conference in 1997, when he was assigned to serve as the Pastor of the Historic St. Paul AME Church on Pittsburgh's Southside. He led this congregation in a period of revitalization and renewal that led to the acquisition of a 16,000 square foot worship complex valued in excess of $1.5 million. In 2002, he was appointed by Bishop Robert Vaughn Webster to serve as the youngest Pastor of the St. James African Methodist Episcopal Church in Pittsburgh's East End. Where he gave tremendous leadership to the Pittsburgh Annual Conference, serving as the Dean of the Board of Examiners, Chair of the Finance Committee, Vice Chair of the Board of Trustees, Chairman of the Board of Directors of the St. James Deaconess Home.

On November 13, 2004, history was made when Dr. Brown was appointed to serve as the Presiding Elder of the Allegheny Scranton District, where he serves as the youngest middle manager in the history of the Pittsburgh Annual Conference, charged with supervising 27 churches and pastors in the Greater Pittsburgh Area. As a presiding elder he has developed many innovative ministries among them are: The adopt a church ministry, One Night Revivals, Fire in the Mountains and the revitalization of the Men's Ministries throughout the district. Currently he is serving as the Treasurer of the Pittsburgh Annual Conference, member of the Trustee Board of the Pittsburgh Annual Conference and Treasurer of the Anderson Adams Restricted Fund.

On the connectional, national and international spectrum, he served as a delegate to the 2004, 2008 and 2012 General Conferences, member of the Credentials Committee, member of the Connectional Council,

Richard Allen Young Adult Council, a member of the Connectional Presiding Elder's Council where he serves on the Finance Committee; 2004-2007 delegate to the National Council of Churches General Assembly, (2004-2011) where he served on the Biotechnology Committee co-authoring the *"Fearfully and Wonderfully Made"* policy statement on Biotechnology. He has represented the AME Church at the 19th World Methodist Conference in Seoul, Korea where he was elected to serve as a member of the Executive Committee and elected to serve on the Worship and Liturgy Commission. He represented the AME Church at the World Methodist Council Meeting in Santiago, Chile.

He is a member of the Board of Trustees of Payne Theological Seminary. In 2004, 2005, 2007, 2008 and 2009 he served as the keynote speaker and lecturer at the German Nation Baptist Convention in Wiesbadan, Germany.

He holds membership in the Wilberforce University, Payne Theological Seminary and Ashland Theological Seminary alumnae associations, Alpha Phi Alpha Fraternity, Incorporated, Prince Hall Masons, Melita Lodge #117. He is a member of St. Cyprian Consistory # 4 A.A.S.R., where he is the Illustrious past Commander in Chief. He was elevated to the coveted 33rd and last degree of Prince Hall Masonry at the 2013 session of the United Supreme Council, Northern Jurisdiction that met in Philadelphia, Pennsylvania. He was selected as one of seven persons nationwide to receive the Religious Heritage of America's Leadership Award. He is also the recipient of the Third Episcopal District Living Witness

Award from the Lay Organization. He has served as the Pastoral Leader for the Hill Top Health Ministries Consortium, President of the Pennsylvania Prison Chaplain's Association. He previously served as the President of the Board of Delegates of Christian Associates of Southwestern Pennsylvania, which is an ecumenical group comprising nine Pennsylvania counties and 20 judicatories and more than one million members. He currently is a member of the Executive Committee and Member of the Board of the Allegheny County Jail Project Committee, The Allegheny County Advisory Board for the Transformation of Senior Centers, as well as numerous other activities that help to improve the quality of life for those in the community.

He has traveled extensively in: Germany, Belgium, Paris, Denmark, Holland, Amsterdam, Jamaica, Mexico, the Czech Republic, Poland, Austria, Sweden, Switzerland, Korea, Australia, Turkey and Lesotho, Southern Africa. and Lyon, France. He has conducted preaching crusades in Paris, France and Berlin, Germany, Lesotho, Southern Africa, Craddock, South Africa and Livingstone, Zambia.

He was formerly employed by the Pennsylvania Department of Corrections as a Facility Chaplaincy Program Director, where he supervised the Protestant, Catholic, Islamic, Native American and Jewish Chaplains. At that time he was the only African American Male to hold that position throughout the Commonwealth of Pennsylvania. In that capacity he led more than 1,000 men to accept Jesus Christ as their personal Savior.

He is married to the former Margo Allen, a native of Burkesville, Kentucky. They are the proud parents of two teenagers, a son, Justin Todd and a daughter, Jordyn Alexis.

Rev. Brown's motto is "Where there is no vision, the people perish". His favorite scripture is: "I had fainted, unless I had believed to see the goodness of the Lord in the land of the living, Wait on the Lord: be of good courage, and he shall strengthen thine heart: wait I say, on the Lord." Psalm 27:13-14

.

DR. ERIC L. BROWN

Made in the USA
Charleston, SC
23 April 2015